PIANO SOLO

RAGTIME GOSPEL CLASSICS

ARRANGED BY
STEVEN K. TEDESCO

ISBN 978-1-4950-1207-5

7777 W. BLUEMOUND RD. P.O. BOX 13819 MILWAUKEE, WI 53213

Visit Hal Leonard Online at
www.halleonard.com

PREFACE

Thank you for purchasing *Ragtime Gospel Classics!* I believe you will find this music to be highly accessible and familiar to your friends, family and church members.

Ragtime has been a favorite style of mine since my early years as a piano student. I later found the ragtime left-hand technique very useful through years of developing my own style of playing in the church. One of the most difficult challenges facing young church pianists is what to do with the left hand. The ragtime left-hand paradigm of roots and fifths alternating with chords provides a solid foundation beneath the melody and yields a lively alternative to the mono-rhythmic style incorporated in most sheet music and hymn books.

These arrangements work well as both solo piano pieces and accompaniments for congregational singing. They are easier to play than most original ragtime compositions, as there is very little usage of octaves and octave passages. Pianists with smaller hands should find them quite playable, though perhaps not without a sufficient degree of practice! For more advanced pianists, octaves may be added in the left hand for an increased level of difficulty.

After you have mastered these arrangements, I invite you to try my previous collection entitled *Ragtime Gospel Hymns* (HL00311763). The arrangements in this volume are more challenging and will serve as a logical next step to a more advanced level of difficulty within the ragtime style.

I hope you enjoy playing these arrangements, and may God bless you, and all those who will hear, as you perform them for His glory!

Steven K. Tedesco

CONTENTS

4 Because He Lives

8 Goodbye World Goodbye

12 He Touched Me

14 I Saw the Light

20 I'll Fly Away

17 Keep on the Firing Line

26 Mansion Over the Hilltop

23 No One Ever Cared for Me Like Jesus

31 There Will Be Peace in the Valley for Me

28 Victory in Jesus

34 What a Day That Will Be

37 Where Could I Go

BECAUSE HE LIVES

A Ragtime Two-Step

Words and Music by WILLIAM J. GAITHER
and GLORIA GAITHER

Arranged by Steven K. Tedesco

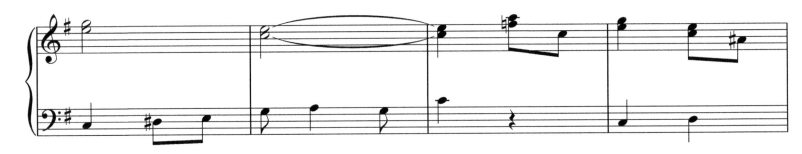

GOODBYE WORLD GOODBYE
A Ragtime Two-Step

Words and Music by MOSIE LISTER
Arranged by Steven K. Tedesco

Not too fast (♩ = 92)

HE TOUCHED ME

A Ragtime Waltz

Words and Music by WILLIAM J. GAITHER
Arranged by Steven K. Tedesco

Slow Waltz tempo ($\quad$ = 80)

I SAW THE LIGHT

A Ragtime Two-Step

Words and Music by HANK WILLIAMS
Arranged by Steven K. Tedesco

Slow March tempo (♩=100)

Dedicated to my father, Gary Tedesco

KEEP ON THE FIRING LINE

A March and Two-Step

Words and Music by J.R. BAXTER, JR.
Arranged by Steven K. Tedesco

I'LL FLY AWAY
A March and Two-Step

Words and Music by ALBERT E. BRUMLEY
Arranged by Steven K. Tedesco

NO ONE EVER CARED FOR ME LIKE JESUS

A Ragtime Two-Step

Words and Music by C.F. WEIGLE
Arranged by Steven K. Tedesco

Slow drag tempo (♩ = 52)

MANSION OVER THE HILLTOP
A Ragtime Slow Drag

Words and Music by IRA F. STANPHILL
Arranged by Steven K. Tedesco

VICTORY IN JESUS
A Ragtime Two-Step

Words and Music by E.M. BARTLETT
Arranged by Steven K. Tedesco

Not too fast (♩ = 88)

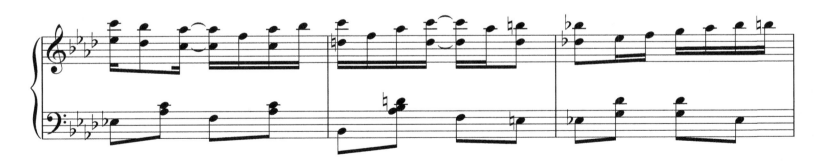

THERE WILL BE PEACE IN THE VALLEY FOR ME

A Ragtime Waltz

Words and Music by THOMAS A. DORSEY
Arranged by Steven K. Tedesco

WHAT A DAY THAT WILL BE
A Ragtime Waltz

Words and Music by JIM HILL
Arranged by Steven K. Tedesco

WHERE COULD I GO
A Ragtime Two-Step

Words and Music by JAMES B. COATS
Arranged by Steven K. Tedesco

Moderate Rag tempo (♩ = 66)

The Best
Sacred Collections
for Piano

Blended Worship Piano Collection

Songs include: Amazing Grace (My Chains Are Gone) • Be Thou My Vision • I Will Rise • Joyful, Joyful, We Adore Thee • Lamb of God • Majesty • Open the Eyes of My Heart • Praise to the Lord, the Almighty • Shout to the Lord • 10,000 Reasons (Bless the Lord) • Worthy Is the Lamb • Your Name • and more.
00293528 Piano Solo $17.99

Hymn Anthology

A beautiful collection of 60 hymns arranged for piano solo, including: Abide with Me • Be Thou My Vision • Come, Thou Fount of Every Blessing • Doxology • For the Beauty of the Earth • God of Grace and God of Glory • Holy, Holy, Holy • It Is Well with My Soul • Joyful, Joyful, We Adore Thee • Let Us Break Bread Together • A Mighty Fortress Is Our God • O God, Our Help in Ages Past • Savior, like a Shepherd Lead Us • To God Be the Glory • What a Friend We Have in Jesus • and more.
00251244 Piano Solo $16.99

The Hymn Collection

arranged by Phillip Keveren

17 beloved hymns expertly and beautifully arranged for solo piano by Phillip Keveren. Includes: All Hail the Power of Jesus' Name • I Love to Tell the Story • I Surrender All • I've Got Peace Like a River • Were You There? • and more.
00311071 Piano Solo $14.99

Hymn Duets

arranged by Phillip Keveren

Includes lovely duet arrangements of: All Creatures of Our God and King • I Surrender All • It Is Well with My Soul • O Sacred Head, Now Wounded • Praise to the Lord, The Almighty • Rejoice, The Lord Is King • and more.
00311544 Piano Duet $14.99

Hymn Medleys

arranged by Phillip Keveren

Great medleys resonate with the human spirit, as do the truths in these moving hymns. Here Phillip Keveren combines 24 timeless favorites into eight lovely medleys for solo piano.
00311349 Piano Solo $14.99

P/V/G = Piano/Vocal/Guitar arrangements.

Prices, contents and availability subject to change without notice.

Hymns for Two

arranged by Carol Klose

12 piano duet arrangements of favorite hymns: Amazing Grace • Be Thou My Vision • Crown Him with Many Crowns • Fairest Lord Jesus • Holy, Holy, Holy • I Need Thee Every Hour • O Worship the King • What a Friend We Have in Jesus • and more.
00290544 Piano Duet $12.99

It Is Well
10 BELOVED HYMNS FOR MEMORIAL SERVICES
arr. John Purifoy

10 peaceful, soul-stirring hymn settings appropriate for memorial services and general worship use. Titles include: Abide with Me • Amazing Grace • Be Still My Soul • For All the Saints • His Eye Is on the Sparrow • In the Garden • It Is Well with My Soul • Like a River Glorious • Rock of Ages • What a Friend We Have in Jesus.
00118920 Piano Solo $12.99

Ragtime Gospel Classics

arr. Steven K. Tedesco

A dozen old-time gospel favorites: Because He Lives • Goodbye World Goodbye • He Touched Me • I Saw the Light • I'll Fly Away • Keep on the Firing Line • Mansion over the Hilltop • No One Ever Cared for Me like Jesus • There Will Be Peace in the Valley for Me • Victory in Jesus • What a Day That Will Be • Where Could I Go.
00142449 Piano Solo $11.99

Ragtime Gospel Hymns

arranged by Steven Tedesco

15 traditional gospel hymns, including: At Calvary • Footsteps of Jesus • Just a Closer Walk with Thee • Leaning on the Everlasting Arms • What a Friend We Have in Jesus • When We All Get to Heaven • and more.
00311763 Piano Solo $10.99

Sacred Classics for Solo Piano

arr. John Purifoy

10 timeless songs of faith, masterfully arranged by John Purifoy. Because He Lives • Easter Song • Glorify Thy Name • Here Am I, Send Me • I'd Rather Have Jesus • Majesty • On Eagle's Wings • There's Something About That Name • We Shall Behold Him • Worthy Is the Lamb.
00141703 Piano Solo $14.99

Raise Your Hands
PIANO SOLOS FOR BLENDED WORSHIP
arr. Heather Sorenson

10 uplifting and worshipful solos crafted by Heather Sorenson. Come Thou Fount, Come Thou King • God of Heaven • Holy Is the Lord (with "Holy, Holy, Holy") • Holy Spirit • I Will Rise • In Christ Alone • Raise Your Hands • Revelation Song • 10,000 Reasons (Bless the Lord) • Your Name (with "All Hail the Power of Jesus' Name").
00231579 Piano Solo $14.99

Seasonal Sunday Solos for Piano

24 blended selections grouped by occasion. Includes: Breath of Heaven (Mary's Song) • Come, Ye Thankful People, Come • Do You Hear What I Hear • God of Our Fathers • In the Name of the Lord • Mary, Did You Know? • Mighty to Save • Spirit of the Living God • The Wonderful Cross • and more.
00311971 Piano Solo $16.99

Sunday Solos for Piano

30 blended selections, perfect for the church pianist. Songs include: All Hail the Power of Jesus' Name • Be Thou My Vision • Great Is the Lord • Here I Am to Worship • Majesty • Open the Eyes of My Heart • and many more.
00311272 Piano Solo $17.99

More Sunday Solos for Piano

A follow-up to *Sunday Solos for Piano*, this collection features 30 more blended selections perfect for the church pianist. Includes: Agnus Dei • Come, Thou Fount of Every Blessing • The Heart of Worship • How Great Thou Art • Immortal, Invisible • O Worship the King • Shout to the Lord • Thy Word • We Fall Down • and more.
00311864 Piano Solo $16.99

Even More Sunday Solos for Piano

30 blended selections, including: Ancient Words • Brethren, We Have Met to Worship • How Great Is Our God • Lead On, O King Eternal • Offering • Savior, Like a Shepherd Lead Us • We Bow Down • Worthy of Worship • and more.
00312098 Piano Solo $16.99

HAL•LEONARD®

www.halleonard.com